IF I COULD PRAY AGAIN

IF I COULD PRAY AGAIN

David A. Redding

WORD BOOKS, PUBLISHERS
WACO, TEXAS

TO MY CHILDREN

Marian Telford
John Maxwell
David Mitchell
Mark McCleery

ACKNOWLEDGMENTS

Frances Cronise Weaver
Sandra Jo Cook
Dorothy McCleery Redding
Helen Loos Whitney
Louise Allen Peters
Phyllis Murphy

Contents

If I Could Pray Again

IF I COULD PRAY AGAIN	15
NO ONE ELSE WILL DO	16
AT THE BEGINNING	17
WHAT NEXT, O GOD?	18
PRAY SENSE	18
A CONFESSION	19
IF I COULD BE MYSELF	20
WHAT IS GOD'S PRAYER?	21
IN EVERY PRAYER OF MINE	22
PRAYER MAKES A DIFFERENCE	23
MAKE ME LIKE NEW AGAIN	24

That Bright Blessing

THIS SMALL REQUEST	29
PUTTING OFF THANKS	29
TWO'S TOO MANY GODS	30
TEACH ME HOW TO GIVE	31
IT IS MORE BLESSED TO LIVE	32
NOT TO BE A BOTTLENECK	32
A STEWARD'S PRAYER	33
THANKS IN SIX STARTS	35
BEFORE SITTING DOWN TO DINNER	38

IN WHOSE NAME WE BREAK THIS
   BREAD   38
FIRST COME, FIRST SERVED   39

I Feel the Chill of Fear

SOMETHING MORE   43
RESPITE   44
SAY A PRAYER FOR PRAYER   44
FORGET YOU NOT   46
NO SECRETS   47
ON THE CHANCE GOD MAY BE IN   48
STEADY   50
BACK TO THE WALL   50
EXTREME UNCTION   51
MY DYING WORDS   53
TO HELP MY FRIEND FACE DEATH   55
I WON'T TAKE NO FOR AN ANSWER   56

The Names and Faces in My Prayers

LET ME REMIND YOU   61
A THANK-YOU NOTE FOR HOME   62
A HUSBAND'S PRAYER FOR HIS WIFE
   DURING CHILDBIRTH   64
GIVE LOVE STRENGTH   66
S. O. S.   67
TO BE SAID AFTER SUCCESS   69
CREATED UNEQUAL   70
TAKING CRITICISM   71
I CANNOT TELL A LIE ANY MORE   72
STOP ME IF YOU'VE HEARD THIS—   74
MOUNTAIN MOVER   76

A CONVALESCENT'S PRAYER 76
FOR THE UP AND OUT 77

Did You Call!

DID YOU CALL? 81
UPON ENTERING CHURCH 82
CHURCH REMINDS ME 83
YOU PROMISED 84
TRANSFIGURATION 85
ORDINATION 86
STOP FOR REPAIRS 87
A PRAYER FOR AMATEURS 88
UNEMPLOYMENT 89
A COMMUNION PRAYER 90
ASK GOD TO SPEAK UP 91
DISTRESS REHEARSAL 92
BACK TOGETHER 93

Star Above My Stable

STAR ABOVE MY STABLE 97
STARLIGHT 98
ADULT ADVENT ANNOUNCEMENT 99
CHRISTMAS COME 100
CHRISTMAS COME AND GO 100
A BETTER IDEA 102
A GIFT FOR A SPECIAL OCCASION 103
A CHRISTMAS CREDIT 104

I Need This Holy Time

LENT IS GOOD FOR SOMETHING 107

A TWO-WAY CONVERSATION   *109*
DON'T GIVE UP GOD FOR LENT   *110*
LENT'S EXPECTING   *111*
MAUNDY THURSDAY NIGHT   *112*
BEFORE GOOD FRIDAY DINNER   *115*
LENT'S LAST PRAYER   *116*
MARY'S EASTER   *117*
EASTER THE WAY IT WAS   *118*

If I Could Pray Again

IF I COULD PRAY AGAIN

If I could pray
Again,
I think I would begin
The way my mother
Taught me—
Beside my bed.
But when I lay me
Down,
I find I can't go back:
The bridge is burned.
I can't go on like this;
The road ahead dead-ends.
My only hope is height.
And yet
I know of nothing new
For that, my Father,
Except to try once more—
Just as I used to do—
Asking inspiration
In this more pressing
Situation;
Remembering You promised
The Kingdom
To those becoming
Like little children once again.
And so I pray You, Lord,
Once more;
Teach me this time
My soul to keep

For others' sake,
As well as Christ's.
O let me sleep
And wake tonight
On that,
'Til prayer comes back
To me.

Amen

NO ONE ELSE WILL DO

O God,
Refresh my memory
With the Good News I already know
About You,
For I keep forgetting it
And have to be reminded
In order to keep it.
And tell me more,
For I know so little.
Show me
How all the fatigue, friction,
And folly of my life
Are not evidence against Your existence,
But proof of my vast need.
If no man
Can talk me into belief,
Let that be one more reason
For my prayer,
A sign
That I shall not be satisfied
With hearsay—
With anything less

Than a word straight from Your lips.
Only You are tall enough
To tower over the horizon
Of my human limitations
And tell me where I am.

Amen

AT THE BEGINNING

O God,
How poor I am. How rich
If I could still have prayer.
O God, how low I am:
My mortal flight is on one floor.
But I am tired of sitting on these chairs,
Homesick for that upper room.
It makes me think of those old altar stairs,
And wonder
If they would still hold my weight.
There was a door up there
He used to keep unlocked;
The latch was low,
And I could always open it
If I got down
Upon my knees.

Amen

WHAT NEXT, O GOD?

We have plans, O God;
We do not have time
To pray,
And cannot think
Of a thing
To say to You,
O God.
You must be merciful—
Who else could bear us,
Or we dare come to?

Amen

PRAY SENSE

O Lord, beside You
I am a mere dream of being;
Forgive me
If I seem to say my prayers
To nobody—
As if I were talking to myself,
Or for some other's benefit;
Teach me how to pray
To Someone Real.

Amen

A CONFESSION

I must confess,
I always put off prayer
'Til last,
To do
What is humanly possible
First.
For it is so much easier
To jump
Than to sit still,
To do it my own way
Than to wait
For Someone Else.
I would rather
Work all day,
Any other way,
Than to do Your will.
Father, forgive me,
For I know
Not what I do.

Amen

IF I COULD BE MYSELF

Thank You, Christ,
For assuming
My sin was something
I did when I was
Not myself.
Make me as one
Of Your hired servants
So I can play the man
You made,
And make up
For a little of the harm
I've done
By not being
Me.

Amen

WHAT IS GOD'S PRAYER?

O God,
You know my prayers
Before I ask them—
What is Your prayer?
You have done so much
For me—
What do You want
Me to do
For You?

O Lord,
I do not have You
In my power,
Pocketed
In this place,
To do my religious pleasure;
The whole world
Is in Your hands.
If I can just remember
How important You are,
My wishes will not matter
So much to me any more.
And I will get
Caught up
In You and Your desire
So far,
I will forget
What I came for,
Lost in the wonder of why
You came
For me.

Amen

IN EVERY PRAYER OF MINE

My Father,
Yours
Is the power,
And my poor prayer
Only a door
Opened to let You in;
But if I ever forget
What You did for me,
Jesus of Nazareth,
Let my tongue cleave
To the roof of my mouth,
And my right arm hang
Useless at my side.
And with Your help,
O Lord, from now on
I shall mention—
In every prayer of mine—
The names of young and old
You lay upon my heart.

Amen

PRAYER MAKES A DIFFERENCE

O Lord,
To whom it is never
Too late to come,
For whom nothing is too much,
Whose miracles always come in time—
Not what is asked for
But called for—
O God,
I pray to You
For blessings that go beyond
My poor prescriptions
To cover my invisible needs.
I enter Your presence
An impossible problem—
Imprisoned in sense,
Set in my ways,
Dead to the world
Of life. Though,
If you are God,
And You are here,
And I draw near
In faith and shame—
How can I ever
Be the same
Again?

Amen

MAKE ME LIKE NEW AGAIN

O God, who made me once,
Make me over new again.
Once is not enough;
Save me today
With more of the same light,
One more degree of glory.
I cannot put my privation into words,
But I have faith at least
That I could have faith,
That I could be better
If I wanted to—
And that the very sight of You
Could make me want to very much.
And I, who cannot pray,
By Your presence could learn
To put one word in front of another
For my feet to follow.

O God,
I do not know what I want,
But You know.
I do not know where I am,
But I know where You are;
Show me the way.
I am here to be helped,
To get back my hope,
To find that illusive happiness
That does not depend on getting
What it wants.
Come back to me, O God,
Lest I forget how good life can be,
What it is to wake up in the morning
Eagerly.
Keep me young,

And help me at the halfway mark
Not to throw away the good I've done.
Keep me from getting weak,
From going to pieces
At the last minute.

O God, I tremble to think
How little I have to show
For my faith
Since youth;
I dare not die in my condition!
Step into my life,
My world,
My house—now—
Before it is too late.
Make my future bright
With fresh goodness and refreshing faith,
That my life may close
On an ascending note
Of joy.

Amen

That Bright Blessing

THIS SMALL REQUEST

O Lord,
That bright blessing,
Which makes it
Possible
For us to be
Ourselves
And to like each other
For what we are,
Is Yours
To bestow;
Grant tonight
This small request
For so great
A God.

Amen

PUTTING OFF THANKS

I pray, my Father,
That You will
Not let me
Put off my thanks
Too long,
For I do not have
All the time
In the world,
As You do.

Do not let me
End up
As one who did
The least
He could get away with—
When You did the most
Anyone could have done,
With a Son.

Amen

TWO'S TOO MANY GODS

Dear God,
Don't let money
Conquer me
By dividing
My attention;
I cannot serve
Two masters.
Make me Your servant,
So everyone who knows me
Will know that
I am Yours,
And You are
My one and only
God.

Amen

TEACH ME HOW TO GIVE

O Lord,
You have taught me how to pray—
Teach me how to give.
Forgive me
If I have hurt anyone
By flinging my silver carelessly
In the face of need,
Or humiliated men
By making them victims
Of my charity.
Help me to give
Out of love,
To give myself,
To know when to give and run
And when to give and keep on giving
'Til the work is done.
Teach me how to add
The finishing touch;
And if it be Your holy will—
The hardest thing of all—
How to give
In the name
Of Christ.

Amen

IT IS MORE BLESSED TO LIVE

I believe,
O Lord,
That it is more blessed
To give
Than to receive—
But to live
That high
Will take another hand-out
From You.

Amen

NOT TO BE A BOTTLENECK

O God,
All my blessings
Are Your business—
Which reminds me of
A world of favors.
Living is like eating
Out of Your hand.
Grant I shall not fail
To look up
Into Your face
With appreciation;
Nor forget
To pass along
The heaping platter
Someone else passed on
To me.

Amen

A STEWARD'S PRAYER

Almighty God,
Make me want to give
Without being made to,
As I do when I watch Your hand
Quicker than the eye,
Paint starry heavens,
Pour out sky,
And across a table
Pass me bread and blood-red wine
By Your Son,
Who was not afraid to die
For You and me.

It is more than I should take—
Could take—
Without tears,
Without wanting to live up to it.
Show me what I have to give, O God;
Show me that my treasure
Of talent, time, and energy
Is not something to hoard
But to invest in others;
That everything I have
Would make a good gift.

Point out to whom I should give
So I won't forget the friends
I have given something to live for—
They are counting on me for more.
Introduce me to those
Dying to have something
I'm dying to give.
Single out my Lazarus for me,
Before it is too late,
Before he has lost his chance
And I have lost my soul.

O God,
Help me to be careful
Not to corrupt charity with my pride;
Keep me from casual giving,
From ever giving
Except from the position
Of prayer—
And only after careful thought,
But always with a little extra,
And from the bottom of my heart.

My Father,
Help me up to see
That giving's such a blessing,
It should be shared—
I must take turnabout
And learn how to be given to,
As You have done.

Amen

THANKS IN SIX STARTS

I

O God,
Help me to be good for others,
So I will do good;
Not to think of my charity
As a favor,
But an honor.
Help me to see that
Though I gave my life,
That would not go beyond the line of duty
But be a small beginning
To Him
Who bought us with a price
That cannot be paid back.

Amen

II

God,
Teach me how to give,
So I will not embarrass
Those who cannot give as much;
Nor humiliate the one to whom I give;
Never to give
So I can give myself credit—
But to give as to God:
To be ashamed it is no more
And I do it no better.

Amen

III

You have coined the word
To give, O God;
Give me the best definition of it

And show me how to use it well
In the complex sentence
Of my life.

Amen

IV

My Father,
Welcome me
Into the household of faith,
And into the company of those
Who know how to give
Out of love.
Help me to take better care of those
Who have been left
Deserted
On the doorstep
Of my heart.

Amen

V

Almighty God,
I hasten to admit,
If ever I have done anything good,
It has not come from my small love
But from above.
And if I've done my best,
By You I'm blest.
Change me, Father,
'Til charity does not seem
So strange a thing for me to do.
Help me to remember
That, from the beginning,
Christians have been breaking custom
With kindness.

Amen

VI

Teacher,
Teach me how to give from prayer,
But freely
And with no strings attached;
To be saint instead of reformer,
To give for joy
And not as strategy,
To lose my life in love,
Not to waste it all
On myself.

Amen

BEFORE SITTING DOWN TO DINNER

O God, help me
Not to eat too much,
Nor too fast; for,
Like a child, I have trouble
Doing anything in moderation.
Forbid that I should be
So foolish as not to enjoy
This blessing, or to believe
It is the best. But let
This meal mean more
Than calories; let the bread
Break sacrament.
For even after dinner,
I hunger and thirst
For righteousness.

Amen

IN WHOSE NAME WE BREAK THIS BREAD

O God,
Grace this table
With Your transforming presence.
We pray for that bread
Which banquets the spirit
And puts a song in the heart.
May this fellowship
Leave space for You
And save seats
For all the sons of want
Who want to come,
Or would,

If we could
Be like Him
In whose name
We break this bread
And drink this cup.

Amen

FIRST COME, FIRST SERVED

Save me from
Trying to help You
After it is too late
And I am too tired
To do You any good.
O God,
What is loyalty
If it is not alert?
Who can find time to give
Himself
If he cannot come
At the first call?
Let me wait
Only upon You.

Amen

I Feel the Chill of Fear

SOMETHING MORE

O God,
I am full
But hungry still,
I am fully clothed
But feel the chill
Of fear.
This is why I'm here—
Because I am about
To believe
Your perfect love
Can cast out
My culprit moan,
And this man shall not live
By bread
Alone.

Amen

RESPITE

O Master Builder,
Build me up
Where I am
Torn down.
Hide me awhile
With You,
Until I can
See straight
And feel like walking
Once more
The strait
And narrow
Path.

Amen

SAY A PRAYER FOR PRAYER

O Lord,
You will have to help me
Pray, for how
Could it be prayer if
Ministers must manage it?
There must be more here
Than meets the eye—
Heaven's not simply sky.
The cries of little children
Refuse to be comforted
With Christmas candy,
And adult heartbreaks
Won't be put off
With platitudes.
I am hungry for bread—

Not like Mother used to make—
The kind
That rises high above.
Break me off the blessing
I cannot begin
To knead by hand.

But, Father,
To be fed
Is not enough.
I must be lead,
There must be Someone—
Bigger than I am—
Who could do better
Than the best brains
To figure out my big problem.
The cliff I'm hanging on
Is vertical;
I could use a Lead Man
With a little longer reach.

Amen

FORGET YOU NOT

I am not
Righteous, God,
But You did something extra for me,
With Your Son,
To save me from my feverish ways.
O God,
I am out of miracles
And come now to ask You to make me some.
Do something
To stop the tragedies
Descending upon me,
Upon my friends and neighbors,
Or give me strength to endure them—
Which would be a miracle.
Show me Job's higher way,
That the agony and bafflement,
Instead of turning me against You,
In bitterness and despair,
May bring me to the door
Of the house of life.

Give me faith, hope,
And the joy no man can take from me,
Before I leave this place,
Before it is too late;
Before this day is lost
In a litter of old Sunday newspapers;
Before souls are lost,
And the church is lost,
And the world is lost,
And I am lost
Because I don't care enough,
And don't believe enough
To go to church and pray much
Any more.

Amen

NO SECRETS

O Father, You alone
Know
How far I have fallen,
And how many times;
I beg forgiveness
Because
I cannot bear myself
Any longer
Without a blessing.
O God, no one
Will take me in
Except You—
No one else
Knows what to do.
That is why I
Bow before You,
Hurt, helpless, holding
The remains
Of Your broken image
In my mortal hands.
Take me from here
In mercy.
Grant my mortifying
Mistakes may make me
Humble, tender,
Anxious to do better.
Keep me from breaking down
And giving up,
By the nearness of Your hand.

Amen

ON THE CHANCE GOD MAY BE IN

Without You,
Father,
Life is not
Worth living.
What's the use,
If I'm just waiting
For the end?
Things can't get much worse
If no one hears
Prayers,
Nor cares what happens
To me.
The best education
Cannot be accredited
In Your absence.
If my cure
Is only temporary,
And everything finally
Comes down
To the stifled cry of panic
Misrepresented
In the hospital corridor
By enamel smiles—
I'm stuck!

But I am a Christian,
Father,
Standing before You here,
Knocking,
With head bared,

On the chance
You may be in,
And I am right
In thinking that the Man
Who carried the heaviest cross
Made no mistake.
I am ready
To believe
He is back,
Beside me now,
Ready to bless us all
At once
With Lent's relief
And Advent's light,
Before we take another step
Into the night.

Amen

STEADY

Steady me
Now, my Father,
With faith that goes
A little farther
Into the night.
Brace my belief,
Make me a good traveler
In rough weather,
So this trouble
I'm having
Will not seem like
The last straw,
Only a mean time.
Show me how to let
My grief
Open up for faith—
Wide enough for the sky
To fall in,
Full of
God.

Amen

BACK TO THE WALL

O
God,
I am up against it
Now.
The trouble is,
My hands
Are tied—

And that is what
Made me think
To pray
To You
Like this.

Amen

EXTREME UNCTION

O God,
The pain now is more
Than I can bear
Without divine assistance.
The wear and tear
Of weariness and fear
Are getting the best of me.
My time is fast running out
And I cannot see a thing
In the darkness ahead of me
To cling to.
I may as well admit,
That I am scared to death.
What's more, my cupboard
Is absolutely bare
Of faith—
That's what drove me
To make this prayer.
Don't let me down,
As I have done to You
So many shameful times;
Have mercy on my soul.
Help me to take
One step at a time,

No questions asked.
Since this is Your show,
Show me how to make my exit
Gracefully.
Be my Partner also,
My Senior in this vast
Assignment,
So I may be able
To gather strength
From the shining sun
Of friends,
And to be of good cheer—
As I've been encouraged to do
By the One who at the end,
So beautifully,
Scaled the wall of solid flesh
And overcame the world.
So help me God.

Amen

MY DYING WORDS

Let my last words
And thoughts
Be loftier,
Father,
Than the things I've said
In the barbershop.
Steel me
To face the music,
As any man would
If he knew he had
A Saviour
Standing by
To forgive the past
And take him by the hand
Into the place
He went to prepare.
Help me to die
Honestly,
Not pretending
Nothing is happening.
Help me to die
In a state
Of excitement,
Not stupor
As befitting
One in the womb.
If there is pain,
Let me remain secure
In the promise
It will not be more
Than I can bear.

If there is fear,
Help me not to forget
That is what Your love is for.
If it is dark,
Remind me
Night must come
Before morning.

And since You've been
So thoughtful
To supply me whatever
I needed,
Up to now,
Help me to go on
Trusting You
To do everything necessary
At the last minute
To take me
On up—
If it is Your will.

Amen

TO HELP MY FRIEND FACE DEATH

Holy Spirit,
I know that sacred words and bowed heads
Cannot invent a prayer,
But You have promised
To intercede for me,
With sighs too deep for tears.
You have never yet
Sent more on a man
Than he could stand,
If he stood by You;
Give my friend something stronger
Than anything I can say or do—
A little something to hold him up,
To help him fight
And never give up
Hope.
Give him some peace and joy
No man nor pain can take away.
Help him not to expect too much
From this life,
But to know he cannot expect too much
From You.
And since he has been
But a hair's breadth from death
Since birth,
Teach him how breathlessly close
He is to life—
If he will become
Like a little child
Again.

Amen

I WON'T TAKE NO FOR AN ANSWER

O God,
Time weighs heavily on my hands
Today,
And life lies flat
In helplessness.
But, good God
Of this world and the next,
Do not let a few minutes
Of suffering
Frighten away
A lifetime of faith.
Do not permit
This awful disappearing act
Death makes us do
To wipe out our next world.
O Worker of Miracles,
Only a miracle can break
The curse of doubt
Descending upon me now.
Reinforce my trembling faith
Before it all falls down.
Help me to remember
That His resurrection
Was made to order
For such a time as this.
And before I get locked up
In that dim view of life
I get from the naked eye,
Help me not to forget
I have a millennium coming—

That my sore eyes
Are still eligible
For a vision of the risen Christ;
My lost soul is not lost
If I will stop right now
And say, "I'm sorry,"
And this time
Not take "No"
For an answer
To the undiscovered.
But, depending
Upon a Better Man
I'll take His word
For it; dying
Believing,
There is much to forgive
But nothing to fear.

Amen

The Names and Faces
in My Prayers

LET ME REMIND YOU

I need You
To bring out
The good side
In me, O God.
Exaggerate
Anything You see
That looks
Like You;
Polish up
Your image
Inside.
Alert me
To my assigned
Battle station.
Train me to see
Names and faces
In my prayers,
As You do;
And accentuate
Anything in me
That reminds You
Of Your Son.

Amen

A THANK-YOU NOTE FOR HOME

O God,
How can I ever thank You enough
For my home?
Of all Your good ideas,
Surely this was one of the most wonderful!
O God, this tells me so much about You.
I feel that in the home
You nearly give away Your plans—
You didn't desert me,
Like a foundling on the earth,
But left me at birth
In the loving arms of mother.
And it is timely today to thank you
First for that home
Where I first saw the light of day.
I cannot bear to think of a life
In solitary confinement,
And I blame myself now
For not counting the blessing it was
To be cradled in affection from the first,
To be led by the hands of brothers and sisters,
And by parents who temporarily took the name of
    "Father,"
In Your place,
Until I learned through them who was.

I thank You for the homes
I was given in marriage;
I tremble before the blessedness
Of being first in another's affections
Until death us do part;

For the privilege of speaking for You
To our children.
I remember the heartwarming
Homes where I was a guest,
Treated as a member of the family,
And thank You for my turn
To be host to someone else.

My mind is teeming today
With the treasures that come tumbling to me
Through the door of home:
The opportunities of teaching, learning,
Giving, receiving,
Loving, being loved;
Of dividing life into husband and wife,
The gift of companionship,
Partners to the end,
And all the wealth of comfort in our children.
Accept my thanks for all this,
For home is herald of the place
From where it came.
Teach me how to live as a child here,
That I may be ready one day
To be Your child there:
How to behave to my brothers,
So I may be able to treat all Your children
As my brothers.
And as I was once taught
To call my earthly parent "Father,"
Teach me how to say, "Our Father,
Who art in heaven,"
Until You have
Your housewarming.

Amen

A HUSBAND'S PRAYER FOR HIS WIFE
DURING CHILDBIRTH

O God,
I call upon You now
To be a tower of defense
To my loving and faithful wife,
That the pain may not be
Beyond her strength.
O God, keep the fear small
And make the time seem short,
That throughout the ordeal
She may remain calm and unafraid.
Hold her hand tightly,
O God,
And take the child from her
Tenderly.
Turn her travail of birth
Quickly
Into the joy of life.

And, O God, as I pray You
To give her life back to her,
Breathe life into the child;
Give him or her good health,
In body, mind, and soul,
Let this child be Your child,
And be a blessing to us all.

O God,
How do I pray
For both mother and child,
That they may suffer no want
For my lack of piety?
Make me better
That I may be better for them,
More deserving of them
And not so ashamed to have
Nor to ask for so much.
Though I am not a righteous man,
Yet, because You are able
To be merciful to me,
And mighty to a mother
And her little one,
Hear my prayer.

Amen.

GIVE LOVE STRENGTH

Pour iron
Into my Christian
Blood, O God.
I do not want
To be hard
Nor go soft.
Give me strength
To be kind
And virtuous;
Friendly
Yet not familiar;
Sympathetic
But not succumbing
To my emotions,
Remaining
In the temptations
Of tenderness and love;
As always,
Your servant.

Amen

S. O. S.

Rescue me
My Lord,
I am your runaway
Slave.
My escape has been
My slavery.
I've been so busy
Making faces,
I've forgotten
Who I am;
And I've been
Embroidering
My life so beautifully
I hadn't noticed
I'd been doing it
On paper
Instead of linen.

Looking up just now
Reminds me
That I'd like to make
An honest living—
But can't remember how.
I know my sleep of sin
Had quite an undertow
To make me so hard
To live with,
And take me out so far
From innocence.
I'm marooned
From meaning,
With only the rind
Of cheap memories
To chew on.

The sore points
Festering unforgiven
Between me
And the other fellow
Have built up
Into swords' points—
So I'm at war
With You
And Yours.

Could you do anything
For me—
With me—
At this point?
I'm just as sick
As You are
Of my alibis,
And prayers
Ad lib.
O bring me back
And bring me in.
Restore the ruins
Of myself,
O Master of the sea
Of men and sin.

Amen

TO BE SAID AFTER SUCCESS

O God,
Let me be Your servant still
In success as in failure.
Let me feel as close
To You
In happiness
As in heartbreak,
Never to be satisfied
So long as there is sorrow
And something I can do
In the name
Of the King
Who took upon Himself
The form
Of a Servant.

Amen

CREATED UNEQUAL

My life is a constant
Reminder:
I am not created equal
To You,
Father in heaven.
My daily breath and bread
Is not enough; my supply
Of patience and understanding
Always falls short
Of the demand.
I simply cannot cope
With any situation
Adequately,
Without more outside
Hope.
My salvation is never
Smugly secure.
I know I can be saved,
Dear Christ,
Only as I remember
My mortality's always an
Operation Shoestring.

Amen

TAKING CRITICISM

My Father,
Make me grateful
For criticism,
For it is nothing
To all I deserve.
Help me to spend it
Wisely on
Soul-searching,
Self-improvement—
To be glad
It is no worse.
And if it is coming
From the cross
I'm carrying for You,
Hear my cry
For more.

Amen

I CANNOT TELL A LIE ANY MORE

I

You know,
Father,
How hard it is
To be
Honest to God
In prayer
When I am not that way
Elsewhere.
But I have to begin
Someplace—
Why not here
In Your house?

II

My dishonesty
Disqualifies my faith,
For how can I believe
That You are trustworthy
If I'm not?
My lies cast aspersions
On You.
Make me a better man
So I will not betray
My trust
In Your Best Man.

O God,
You know
I'm no good,
The way I am,
Perpetuating
Sham.
I'm so artificial,
I can't communicate.
I have never met
My wife,
Nor the children,
Except in passing
Comments
On the weather,
Or passing out
Last-minute presents
Of model ships
Squeezed in
On tight week ends.
Hearts don't break
Any more;
They're drying up
In drugs and decaying
In indifference—
Tranquilized, not
Tranquil.

IV

Father,
I would like
One more try
To be
Myself.

Give me courage
To give encouragement
In patience,
And understanding
To make myself plain
So I can sign off
At last, "Sincerely Yours,"
And You and I
Can look back and forth—
Man and Maker,
Face to face
On solid ground.

Amen

STOP ME IF YOU'VE HEARD THIS—

Stop me,
Father,
If you've heard this before.
I don't have time
To fool You any more.
Get me off
This dirty train
Of thought
Before it runs away
With me.
Lay Your hand
Upon my shoulder
Of self-indulgence.
Prune the unfruitful vines
In my mind
And prevent

The stampeding
Jungle growth of greed
And lust
From choking me.

O God,
I've gone against the grain
Of Your good will
So long,
You may not recognize
Me now.
I'm not the man
I was,
Nor the man You meant.
You have the picture—
Break it up.
Give me a second chance
To start all over—
You did it for Francis
And for a worthless thief—
Please listen
To my prayer.
It's no use for me to
Talk with anyone else
Except You.

Amen

MOUNTAIN MOVER

God, who made earth and heaven,
Day and night,
Minister to the lump in the throat
This morning,
And to those eating their hearts out
In disappointment.
Remember at this moment those
So tired or in such agony,
They feel like quitting.
Assist some young man
Through the knothole of his nightmare.
Use Your cross to cut me
From the knife
Of my complaining,
And in the busy body of my death
Breath Your most holy life.

Amen

A CONVALESCENT'S PRAYER

Forgive me
For the pagan courtesy
Of thanking lucky stars;
Or if I overpaid the doctor
And the pill
With my appreciation,
And forgot to pray to You,
Standing right beside my bed
So silently,
My great Physician.

Amen

FOR THE UP AND OUT

O God,
Anyone can pray
For the down and out;
Give me more charity
Until I can pray for my betters,
Or those in competition with me.
Lead me, Lord, lest
In dredging ditches
I overlook Levites, priests,
And overprivileged people
Suffering in success
And sterile lovelessness.
Someone should pray for those
Damned to popularity
And cheap satisfactions—
Tonight, Father, my heart
Goes out to the ones who also ran;
Whose illness has not been
Dramatic enough
To solicit special attention;
The sheep not black, but graying
Into the background;
That with Your blessing
And my good will,
They may not miss
The miracle.

Amen

Did You Call?

DID YOU CALL?

Was that You
Who called,
O God?
Why did You
Want me
To come
To church
Today?
To pray—
As if I didn't
Know.
What did You
Have in mind
For me?
As if I could
Pretend
I'm deaf and dumb
And blind.

Amen

UPON ENTERING CHURCH

Saviour,
Show us how to put our faith together
On Sunday morning,
For none of us has enough
Alone.
Make this the place
Where we pool our light
To see You better.
Let smiles run easily here
Along the row,
From face to face,
And prayers leap quickly
To our lips
For the stranger
Sitting next to us—
As Christ would do,
Were He sitting
In our pew.
Don't let us forget
To say a word for those
Who couldn't come today—
And others
Who didn't care to,
Who couldn't bear our cold shoulder
Any longer,
Nor the boredom
Of the sermon.
Our Father,
We don't need any defense
For what we're doing here—
If You are prominent
Among those present.

Amen

CHURCH REMINDS ME

O silent Spirit!
Thank You
For the gentle reminders
That fill the years.
It all comes back to me now:
The vows of discipleship
Taken down front,
Under the peace of this roof;
Those promises that trembled
Between man and wife,
The bells that rang for them;
The last rites—
Not something dreaded
That we want to forget,
But to draw strength from
Again.
What a mighty fortress
This has been!

O Father,
May our fathers—
Who by a few precious moments
In this place
Were kept from temptation,
Who found something here
To calm their fear—
Bless us at this moment
With fresh courage,
More faith in the faith;
We too might still be saved.
And if it be Your holy will,
Give us the strong impression
It could happen
In this hour.

Amen

YOU PROMISED

We have no right
To ask
For the bright
Pleasure of Your company,
Blessed God,
But You promised—
And Your ideas
Are so much better than
The ones we pick out
For ourselves.
We would improve so much,
Making these decisions
With Your Hand upon our head.
We think our dying faith
Might still revive,
And that dead hope come back
Alive,
If only You were here.
Our belief in You is buried
Under such a heavy load
Of care and cloud;
We wish that You would
Shout to us the way
You did to Lazarus lying dead.
This evening, make a call upon us all—
The way You said
You always would,
When we were two
Or more, meeting
In Your name.

Amen

TRANSFIGURATION

God,
These words
Are in the vernacular;
Charge them
With Your weight
Of glory.
We breathe
The same old air;
Make it heavy
This morning
With Your loving care.
Surround us now
With all the wealth
Of treasured associations:
Of saints praying
And sinners weeping,
The martyrs and apostles
Who saved the church
And sent it on its way.
May these memories
Steady us
And fertilize our faith,
That we may not fail
When You call
Upon us to play our part
In that golden chain-reaction
Still streaming,
Shining,
From the splendor
Of Your Servant,
Christ.

Amen

ORDINATION

Holy Spirit,
Pour down upon
Laymen
A power not professional.
This church could use
Another hand or two,
If it is to be
The body of Christ.

Amen

STOP FOR REPAIRS

O Lord,
Lift the oppression
Of self-concern that
Settles on us overnight.
Goodness is so slippery—
We keep losing our grip.
You grab hold of us,
We give up.
Great Physician,
Our shoulders are not broad enough
To bear despair.
We need more backbone,
More spring in our step of faith.
Put some peace into us,
So we can
Leave this house like new,
Better able to bear the Good News to others
In more desperate straits.
Help us to be friends first,
And be the first
To make up.
Embrace us again, O God,
Before we go, that we
May go back to work
Happy as kings, because
We are not afraid to be beggars
Before Your mercy seat.

Amen

A PRAYER FOR AMATEURS

O impartial God,
Grant we may all
Gain consciousness
Immediately
Of the staggering confidence
Christ had in His friends.
We marvel that
In a world of Greek scholarship
Jesus went down to the sea
To get His men.
In a church grown professional,
Help us to remember
Peter and John;
Teach us how to pray,
Not for specialists but for soldiers,
For saints rather than experts.

O God, we could use good men,
Men of good will,
Better than degrees and decorations.
We are low on patience,
Understanding, and tenderness—
We need men who will dare
To identify with Christ over Aristotle;
Men who seek not merely for knowledge
But for righteousness.
Send us some such amateurs
So that the ministry of a Master
To the sick,
The outcast,
The stranger,
The least of these,
And the little children,
May be remembered and obeyed.

Amen

UNEMPLOYMENT

O save,
O save us,
In such excitement
Others now in bed
Will wish they had been
Here
With us to pray
This hour.
Save this service
From any minister
Trying to run
A one-man show,
Or from members sleeping
Because they don't know
How much they count
When they take time
To bow the knee.
Forgive us for the blasphemy
Of believing from the back seat
Nothing much is going to happen
In church.
Forgive us,
For our memory is very faint
Of Him who promised
We could move mountains
With a mustard seed
Of faith.

Amen

A COMMUNION PRAYER

O God,
How can I reply
To this invitation?
Who am I to deserve
The life-giving bread
And be served wine
That makes a man
Not to thirst again?

O God,
That cross seems so prohibitive
A cost
To pay for me.

Amen

ASK GOD TO SPEAK UP

Dear God,
Please answer "present"
To our call to prayer today,
More audibly than usual.
Speak up enough to wake
The dead, and make the deaf
Hear the word of life You said.
Break the Good News to us
Ever so gently and firmly this time;
Break through our old
Defenses and disarm·us
Completely. Store our souls
With a week's provisions.
We do not need repairs but
To be made over new. That's why
We have come to You.
We do not want
To waste Your precious time;
Make the most of it, O God, this morning—
So You will think Your hour
Well spent, and we can prove it
By the way we go away
From here,
More truly Yours.

Amen

DISTRESS REHEARSAL

We need
A good hour's practice
In this holy place
To make it practical.
Make our guests
Feel the importance
Of Your presence.
Let ministers
Find their place
Beneath the cross,
That we may steal a march
This morning
In this mad race
With death.
Help us
To feel our way
Today,
To the length
Your grace will go,
So we shall know
What's up
When we are having
One of those days
When we need it
Most.

Amen

BACK TOGETHER

O God
Of all the encircling years,
Take me in again
Where You left off
The last time
I left You.
What am I supposed to do
Down here, unless it is
To get to know You?
But there isn't any room,
Or time,
Until You put down
That great "almighty me"
Taking up Your place.
Give me grace
To make the sacrifice
Of self
So necessary to my neighbor's
Happiness,
And to my own
Salvation.
Let this prayer be the signal
To begin,
Before another Sunday
Finds me the same old way
Again.

Amen

Star Above My Stable

STAR ABOVE MY STABLE

Please, Father,
Break this habit
Of sin,
Before it's too late
For me to be
Your son.
Drive out the devils
Of lust,
The illicit longings
That have my thoughts
Bewitched.
Don't leave me,
God,
In the present company
Of these dog-desires;
Don't let me linger
In the forbidden territory
Of temptation,
Seducing everything
That comes to mind,
Sacrificing nothing.
Visit my stable.
I have seen Your star
Shining so far
Above me;
And how I long to be
A Bethlehem.

Amen

STARLIGHT

O Lord,
Turn on the light—
The light above Bethlehem.
Let it shine again
Into my darkened heart
At Advent time.
It would be only fair
For You to give me
A star.
I am not so wise;
I am getting cold.
O tell me, Christ,
Where You are now.

Amen

ADULT ADVENT ANNOUNCEMENT

O Lord,
Let Advent begin again
In men,
Not merely in commercials;
For that first Christmas was not
Simply for children,
But for the
Wise and the strong.
It was
Crowded around that cradle,
With kings kneeling.
Speak to us
Who seek an adult seat this year.
Help us to realize,
As we fill stockings,
Christmas is mainly
For the old folks—
Bent backs
And tired eyes
Need relief and light
A little more.
No wonder
It was grown-ups
Who were the first
To notice
Such a star.

Amen

CHRISTMAS COME

God,
Christmas
Has come
Again.
Before it gets away
While we are sleeping
It off,
Give us the grace
To come
To Christmas.

Amen

CHRISTMAS COME AND GO

Here comes Christmas again,
So soon;
It seems only yesterday
I remember coming down
The Christmas stairs,
For the first time,
To open stockings
Stuffed for me
By loving hands
Now lost and still.
Precious memories
Of years gone by
Unman me now
And make me wonder
Why they loved me so—

Unless there's something
To it,
And You're behind it,
Moving heaven and earth
Closer
Christmas by Christmas.

Where has the time gone?
How many more are left?
I am afraid to ask,
"How am I doing?"
For this is Your Son's
Birthday;
But I've always been
On the receiving end.
Give me something this year
To remember Christmas by—
Something better than I got
By being one year older.
Since I have had so much,
Since I celebrate One
Who gave and gave,
Since there's not enough
To go around—
Skip me once
So I may learn how
To make a sacrifice
For someone who has
Never had a turn,
Up to now.
Grant me grace
Before it's too late
And I am at somebody's throat,
Missing the time of my life.

Amen

A BETTER IDEA

Father in heaven,
I cannot afford to live
Very far from You,
For I am not very well,
Nor very good,
Without a God like Christ's
To stop by often.
Save me from making
The common mistake of dying
From trying to be my own
Blind guide.

Keep me from sinking
To some low form
Of parasite life
That eats unconsciously,
Irresponsibly,
Out of Your hand.
I do not want to make
A fool of myself—
In front of the mirror,
Or behind my make-up.

Isn't it about time, O God,
That this belief began
To affect my behavior,
And I gave You some relief
From carrying all the load
Alone? O God,
I want You to save the world—
Since You have to start
Some place,
Give me the grace
To let You start with me.

Save me from the wrong spirit,
As from the wrong things;
From being consumed
By irrelevant interests
And from stewing over
Unimportant issues.
Let me save my breath,
My strength, for something
You might like me to do—
With my whole heart—
This Christmas.

Amen

A GIFT FOR A SPECIAL OCCASION

Heaven help me
To think of something
Good enough to give
At a time like this.
Christmas calls for more
Than usual—
Not something simply
Lying around the house,
Nor deposited in the bank—
Something nearer,
Clearer,
Such as
In my mirror.

Amen

A CHRISTMAS CREDIT

O God,
Who thought of Christmas first,
And looked forward to it
From the first new year;
Who, when we fell,
Knew just what we needed—
We look forward
This Christmas
To Your coming back,
For the last time,
On that day
When all creation is finished,
And what was lost in Eden found;
For heaven's
Coming home to earth!

Amen

I Need This Holy Time

LENT IS GOOD FOR SOMETHING

O Lord,
I remember tonight
That all Lent is good for
Is to repent.
Forbid that I
Should be so dead to sin
I cannot see why
I need this holy time
So desperately.
Something in me cries out:
You will not let me be
Content in hell,
Or leading a dog's life,
Slyly, in a silver lining.

Shine Your light
Brightly upon my darkened heart,
That I may see well enough,
O Christ, to search my soul;
And fill up these forty days
With forgiveness for me, so
I won't try to fool myself
Any more.

Let some special blessing
Descend
During these promising days
Upon those dear to me
And dear to You,
O God.

Keep Your promise to everyone
Who prays.
Begin again
The work of grace crying
To be done in me.
Don't forget that heartbreak
I told You about,
And get me
Into the right spirit in time
For Easter.

Amen

A TWO-WAY CONVERSATION

O God,
I am grateful
You live so near,
I do not have to shout.
The holiest week is here;
No need to beg,
For You are quick to
Come at the first call,
And kind enough to stay
And see me through.
Forgive me, too, for never
Getting to the point
You're waiting for me to bring up;
For passing up the cross
Of Christ and rationalizing
Away the painful contrast between
His life and mine;
For being so dizzy with today's details,
I'm hazy on commandments
And careless of His Kingdom.
Please go ahead and dominate
The conversation tonight.
O God,
Make the silence eloquent
With Your thoughts and Your ways;
And make them mine,
For Christ's sake.

Amen

DON'T GIVE UP GOD FOR LENT

O God,
Prevent me from prayer
Unless I intend to take it seriously,
And to expect results;
Help me to handle prayer
As I would high explosives,
Not as child's play.
Someone's waiting, dying for me
To say a prayer.
Help me to pray to win—to pound
And pull at Your heartstrings
Until the door of heaven comes off
And the power's pouring down
With enough miracles
To make the bare hard ground
Green with new-found life again.

Amen

LENT'S EXPECTING

O God,
I have been going on and on
As if I were a machine;
Help me to be
A human being.
Slow me down
To sanity
Before life comes
To a grinding halt.
I have been scraping away
In a dust bowl,
Dying from the dregs
In this dry canteen.
Where did You put my cup
That runneth over?

Amen

MAUNDY THURSDAY NIGHT

At suppertime
Our Father,
We thank You for Your Son,
Who came to earth just in time—
And in the only way to save us—
Who in the jaws of death
And doublecross
Thought only of us;
Who in the emergency of His last night
Characteristically gave us something
To remember Him by;
Gave us every bit of the little time
He had left;
Gave us His last bite
To make us a banquet
To last 'til He came back.

O God, help us,
To see this Last Supper
As for the first time.
Let the intervening centuries
Disappear
Before the desperation
We have in common
With the oldest disciples—
Because time alone
Cannot come between
Man and You.

Have mercy upon us, O God,
If we are here tonight
Out of duty, habit,
Or on any half-hearted pretext,
When we are here really
By royal invitation—
Our places bought with a price
That ought to make us tremble.
O God, we are here
Because we are starving;
Something is missing
On our beautifully printed menus.

O God, we are here
Because we want to be forgiven.
We must confess
We have a burning, craving, for it.
Help us, O God,
To find it in our hearts to say,
"I'm sorry," to each other—
And to You.

O God, we are still here
Because we are lonely:
At night,
At death,
No one can completely understand us—
We cannot understand ourselves.
Our own crowded table is empty,
The conversation deadly,
The company depressing,
The house empty.
Our life echoes like a hollow cave—
We are homesick,
Poor—
Without the wealth
Of Your transforming presence.

O God, we are here, still,
Because we are afraid
We are happy in hell.
Lord, to whom shall we go?
You, Lord, have the words
Of eternal life.

O God, we are staying here
Because we are unhappy
Without You.
Like children,
We want to be where You are;
To feast our eyes on You.
That is our sip of peace,
Our taste of joy.

Amen

BEFORE GOOD FRIDAY DINNER

If this moment of quiet
Is prayer,
If this week is holy
And this Friday good,
Father,
I know
It is not by any order of service
Or a nod of the head,
But by Your mercy—
Which makes me man enough
To admit I am not God—
And by Your Son—
Who taught me always to pray
And not lose heart.

I have taken the time now;
Make it mean something more
Than I can make out of it.
May I remember this moment,
Not as a time when I spoke to You,
But as a place when time stood still
To let You speak to me.
May this meal tonight make vivid
The things for which that Last Supper stood,
And help me not to forget
That this day
Makes
The difference
Between life and death.

Amen

LENT'S LAST PRAYER

O Lord,
Let not Lent leave
Empty-handed—not until
We've poured in all our pent-up
Repentance and powerlessness,
Poured out our heart.
O God, don't let anyone give up now;
Lead him back to prayer
Like a little child.
Lift up
Those who have lain down;
Turn back those who have
Turned their faces to the wall,
With the call
That life's not over yet.
Lent's not finished with us.
Press us to Your breast again,
O Christ, that we may get back
Into the fight for manhood—
More faithful, from this day forward,
To say our prayers to You
Whose love and tender mercy
Do not stop
As long as there is still time
And there is one
Lost sheep.

Amen

MARY'S EASTER

O God,
What if Easter isn't true
For us?
What if we miss it,
As most missed it,
At first,
For lack of faith?
O God, even the disciples
Decided that the women
Told an "idle tale"—
Until their turn came.
Don't forget us,
Our Father, for
We are next,
And we will need
A little extra
Evidence—no,
Not as much
As Thomas.
Just tell us,
In our words,
What You told
Mary.

Amen

EASTER THE WAY IT WAS

O God,
What I would not give
To have Easter back
The way it was,
Before I damaged it
With doubt;
For I do not want
Anything for Easter—
Only Easter. O God,
If once
I could come
Without sitting in judgment
On this old, old story,
But appreciate it.
At times I can see
How silly it is for me,
So blind,
To smile at eyes
That were opened.
Perhaps, with a little help,
I could assume St. John
Is quite as bright as I.
Maybe Handel's Messiah
Doesn't need to be analyzed
To pieces.
Show me how to enjoy
Scripture's mighty music,
Finally,
Not as impertinent scholar
But as penitent.

Allow me to keep
What good sense I've won,
But give me back
The wonder of childhood,
So I won't resent Your keeping
Some facts back—
Since Easter is supposed to be
A surprise.

Amen